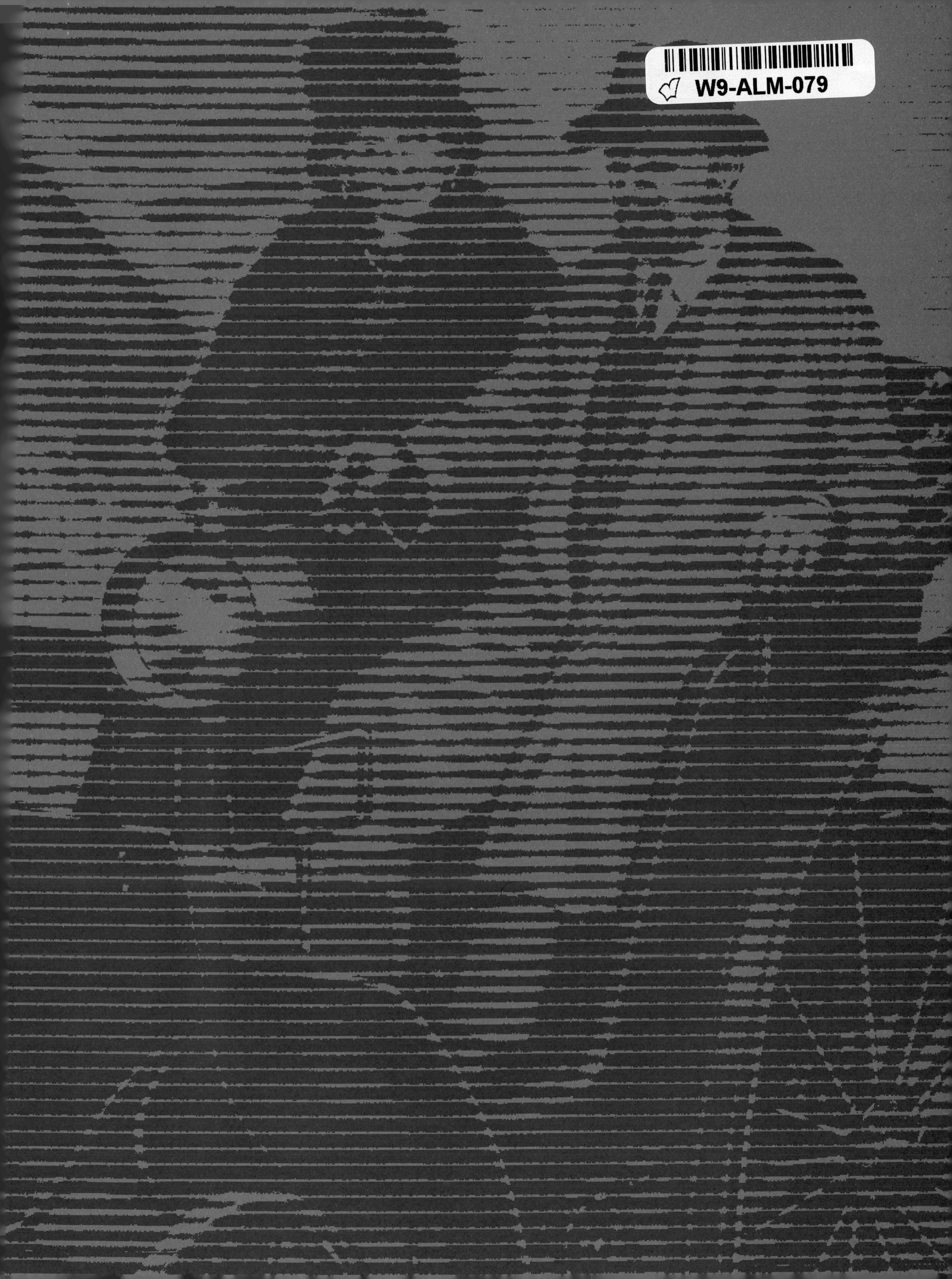

Past and Present

CARS

Neil Morris

Thameside Press

Introduction

Motor cars were first seen on the roads towards the end of the nineteenth century. They were not created by one single person. Many inventors and engineers played a part in their development.

▲ Enjoying a drive in 1922.

◄ Traffic jams are common on our roads today.

▼ New cars are launched all the time.

Rapid growth

The very first cars were driven by steam, but engines soon ran on **gasoline**. At first motor cars were owned only by rich people. Then mass production in factories made cars more affordable. As more people bought cars, they relied less on other forms of transport, such as trains.

The car takes over

In recent years road traffic has built up everywhere, causing jams and **polluting** the air with **exhaust** fumes. Many cities have been forced to create car-free zones, and manufacturers are looking at new forms of energy for cars. A hundred years ago, people had no idea that after 2000 factories would be making millions of new cars every year.

The first cars

People first traveled in gasoline-driven cars at the end of the nineteenth century. But inventors had dreamed of building a "horseless carriage" for a long time before that.

Karl Benz launched his first four-wheeler in 1893. It had an upright steering handle and hard, solid tires.

Steam, gas, and oil

A French **engineer** built a three-wheeled steam tractor as early as 1769. But three German engineers were separate inventors of the car. In 1876, Nikolaus Otto made an engine that ran on coal gas. Then, in 1885, Karl Benz built the first car to go on sale to the public. Gottlieb Daimler developed his own gasoline engine, and in 1895 he too started building cars. The motoring age had begun.

Around the world

Cars spread rapidly. A French car of the 1890s was the first to have its engine at the front. In the U.S., the Duryea brothers built their first car in 1893. Three years later, their company sold 13 automobiles, which they thought was a lot!

◄ Karl Benz (1844–1929), driving his three-wheeler in 1886. It had a very simple engine, which used a chain to drive the back wheels. The car's top speed was 8 miiles per hour.

► The very first Mercedes car of 1901. It was designed by Daimler's partner, Wilhelm Maybach. The car was named after Mercedes Jellinek, the daughter of an Austro-Hungarian **diplomat** who raced Daimler cars.

Leading the way

In Britain, early cars had a person walking ahead with a red flag to warn other road-users that a car was coming.

▲ Early cars had horns which the driver squeezed to make a loud tooting sound.

Mass production

Early cars were individually designed by an engineer and built by craftsmen. This made them very expensive. The growing American motor industry soon changed things.

The Model T Ford was nicknamed "Tin Lizzie." Early models were started by turning a **crank handle** at the front.

Difficult conditions

In the early days, motoring was uncomfortable. Driver and passengers were usually open to the wind and rain. And when it was dry, roads threw up clouds of dust. Cars were also very expensive, both to buy and to keep running well.

New methods

Henry Ford wanted to solve these problems. In 1908, his Ford Motor Company launched its Model T in the U.S. Five years later, the car was selling so well that Ford put a moving **assembly line** into his factory. This meant he could produce more cars more cheaply. Before long, Model T cars were also being made in Britain, Germany, and France.

► At each stage of the moving Ford assembly line, a worker added another part. The factory could produce a complete car in about an hour and a half.

◄ Henry Ford (1863–1947) sits in one of his cars with his son, Edsel.

Driver's seat
The front of a Model T Ford looked very different from today's cars. There was no real dashboard and there were only two forward **gears**.

steering wheel

fold-up windscreen

throttle control

hand brake

forward clutch

reverse clutch

light

brake

▼ The Renault AX first took to French roads in 1908. Louis Renault (1877–1944) was a famous car manufacturer.

▲ Air-filled tires were first put on French cars in 1895 by the Michelin brothers. Steel wheels (above) soon replaced wood. Wire spokes (top) came in during the 1920s.

► Heavy traffic in London, England, in 1912. There are no road signs. Policemen did their best to direct the traffic.

Motoring in luxury

Henry Ford built cars that ordinary working people could afford. But some smaller car manufacturers concentrated more on comfort and style.

The Rolls-Royce Phantom II came out in 1930. Its engine was six times more powerful than the Model T Ford.

Rolls and Royce

English engineer Henry Royce built his own car in the early 1900s. Then he met Charles Rolls, who sold cars. The two men formed a company called Rolls-Royce, and in 1907 they built their famous Silver Ghost. Many called it the best car in the world.

Trained chauffeurs

By the 1930s, rich people often had more than one car, as many people do today. They hired trained, uniformed **chauffeurs** to drive them in their large luxurious cars. The chauffeurs also looked after the cars and cleaned them.

◀ Bugatti was one of the most famous makes of luxury car in the 1930s. The company also made racing cars.

BUGATTI

▶ Companies use the world's motor shows to launch their new models to the press and the public. This is the Paris motor show of 1929.

▲ The dashboard and controls of this 1935 Mercedes were designed to look stylish as well as practical.

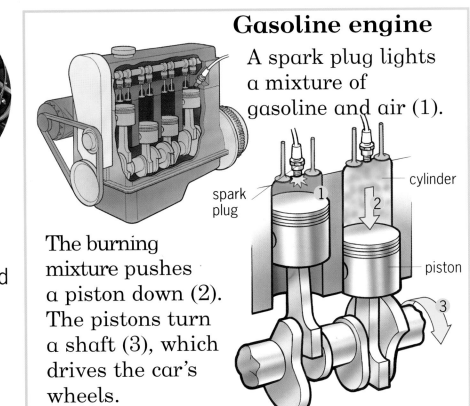

Gasoline engine

A spark plug lights a mixture of gasoline and air (1).

The burning mixture pushes a piston down (2). The pistons turn a shaft (3), which drives the car's wheels.

spark plug

cylinder

piston

◄ The 1935 car Auburn Speedster was ideal for movie stars. It had a special locker for golf clubs, as well as a fitted radio, which was rare at the time.

Cars for the people

In the 1930s, a German company created a "people's car." It was not luxurious and was nicknamed the Beetle, but it went on to become the best-selling car of all time.

The Volkswagen Beetle had its engine at the back. The trunk, or luggage space, was at the front.

Volkswagen and Porsche

In the early 1930s, the German dictator, Adolf Hitler, wanted a car made that every worker could afford. In 1934, the first Volkswagen – German for "people's car" – was designed by Ferdinand Porsche, who later became famous for his sports cars.

World best seller

After the war, more and more Beetles were produced. By 1965 the figure was over a million a year, and they sold all over the world. Altogether, more than 21 million Beetles have been made. The German factory no longer makes them, but they are still produced in South America.

Gears

Gears change the speed of a car's wheels.

shaft from engine

small gearwheel

shaft to wheel

A

big gearwheel

B

C

D

In first gear (A), a small **gearwheel** turns a big one. The car's wheels turn slowly. (B) shows second gear. In fourth gear (C), the two gearwheels turn at the same speed. Reverse gear (D) has a third gearwheel.

▶ The British Mini was launched in 1959. It packed everything a city car needed into a very small space. Even the wheels were small.

MARY QUANT COLOUR SHOP

CARNABY ST.

▲ Before flashing **turn signals**, the yellow arm swung out to show the car was going to turn.

► In the 1950s and 1960s, many American cars, such as Cadillacs, were very big and brightly colored. The fins at the back were added just for show.

▲ In 1936, the Fiat Topolino was the smallest mass-produced car in the world.

Chicago

New York

Los Angeles

▲ As more cars were built, they needed more fast roads. In the U.S., roads linked up right across the country. The yellow roads are called interstate highways.

Supercars

Some drivers have always been more interested in speed and style than in simply traveling from one place to another. Fast, expensive supercars were made for them.

The Ferrari Testarossa (Italian for "red head") was launched in 1984. It has a top speed of 180 miles per hour.

Motor racing

The first motor race took place in France in 1894. By the 1920s, sports cars could reach 100 miles per hour, and car companies realized that success in races helped sell their road cars. Alfa Romeo, Bentley, and Bugatti all made racing cars which were among the best in the world.

Italian style

Enzo Ferrari was a racing driver for Alfa Romeo. In 1929, he founded his own car company (Ferrari). He used all the knowledge he gained as a racing driver to make stylish sports cars. The Testarossa was just one of these.

Quick change

When racing cars stop at the pits, they change tires and fill up with gasoline very quickly. A large crew of helpers tries to get this done in less than ten seconds.

1 lifts up the back end.
2 lifts up the front end.
3 takes off and puts on wheel nuts.
4 takes off the old wheel.
5 puts on the new wheel.
6 puts in gasoline.
7 holds the fuel pipe.
8 has a fire extinguisher ready.
9 turns the gasoline pump on and off.
10 cleans the driver's **visor.**
11 shows instructions to the driver.

▲ Many sports car manufacturers build racing cars too. The famous red Ferraris have had many great drivers, such as Niki Lauda (top) and Michael Schumacher (above).

◄ Tires usually have grooves that help grip the road. Some racing cars use smooth tires, called slicks, when the track is dry.

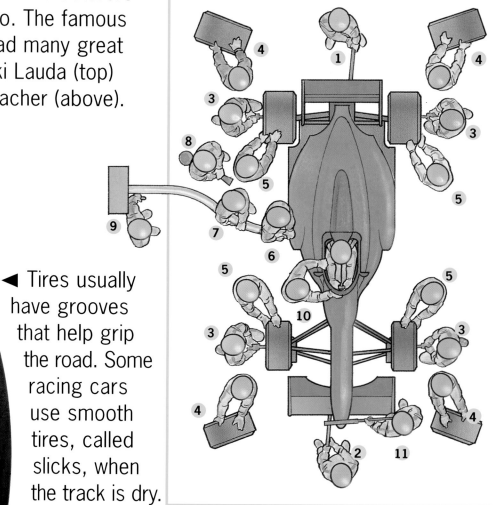

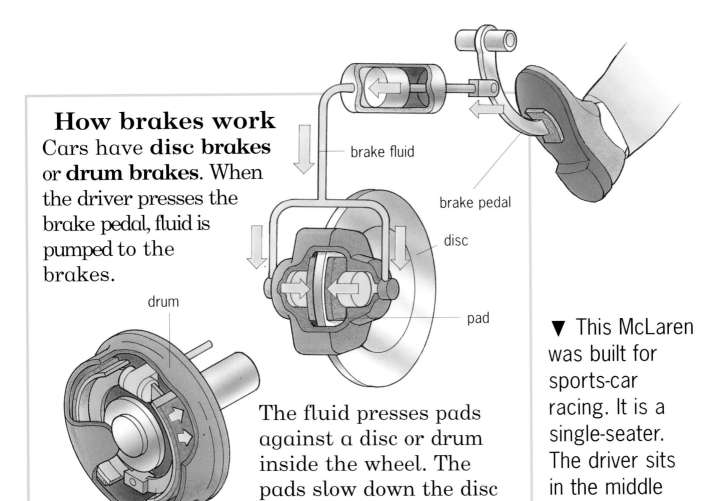

How brakes work

Cars have **disc brakes** or **drum brakes**. When the driver presses the brake pedal, fluid is pumped to the brakes.

brake fluid

brake pedal

disc

pad

drum

pad

The fluid presses pads against a disc or drum inside the wheel. The pads slow down the disc or drum, and the wheels go slower, too.

▼ This McLaren was built for sports-car racing. It is a single-seater. The driver sits in the middle of the car.

Modern technology

Compared with the early days of motoring, car travel today is a lot more comfortable.

Multi-purpose vehicles came out in the 1990s. Called minivans or people-carriers, they can carry many passengers.

New developments

Exhaust fumes harm people and the environment. New cars run on **unleaded gasoline** and have systems to stop some of the fumes. But many car journeys are still made by people on their own, which is a waste of energy. Minivans can help with this problem, when families and friends travel together.

Into the future

In the twenty-first century, people are looking for new ways to save energy. Perhaps gasoline will be replaced by other forms of energy for cars. The first 100 years of motoring were an exciting period of travel, and cars might change as much again in coming years.

Crash testing

Dummies are used as drivers and passengers, to test the safety of cars. In the car on the left, the dummy driver is protected by an airbag. The pictures below show how the airbag works.

1 The airbag is stored in the middle of the steering wheel.

2 In a crash, the bag bursts out and fills with air.

3 The airbag protects the driver by forming a soft pillow.

▶ In this Jeep, all four wheels are driven by the engine. This gives the car extra grip, especially on rough, hilly ground.

◄ Factories still use the assembly line system. But today, many workers have been replaced by **computerized** robots.

▼ Computers are also used by car designers. They can help develop the best shape for new models.

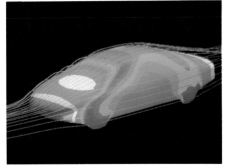

► Cars can use electricity instead of gasoline. They have to have their batteries regularly re-charged, as shown here.

Glossary

assembly line
A line of workers in a factory who put together a car.

chauffeur A person employed by someone to drive them in their car.

computerized
Controlled by a computer.

crank handle
A handle which early motorists had to turn to start their car.

diplomat An official who represents their country abroad.

disc brake
A brake that slows down the car by pressing pads against a disc inside the wheel.

drum brake
A brake that slows down the car by pressing pads against a drum inside the wheel.

engineer A person who designs and builds cars and other machines.

exhaust Waste gases that are given off by a car's engine.

gasoline A liquid made from oil that is burned in the engine to make a car go.

gear A set of toothed wheels that change the speed of a car's driving wheels.

gearwheels
A toothed wheel that fits into another toothed wheel and turns it.

multi-purpose vehicle A large car with a lot of room for carrying many passengers.

pollute To damage the air and the environment with poisonous and harmful substances.

turn signal
A flashing light on a car that shows which way it is going to turn.

unleaded gasoline Gasoline that does not contain the metal lead and so causes less harm to the environment.

visor The see-through part of a crash helmet which covers and protects the driver's eyes.

Index